READY
FOR THE
KING

A JOURNEY TO THE HEART OF JESUS TO PREPARE FOR HIS RETURN

CATHERINE M. VITETTA

Ready for the King, Paperback
Copyright © 2023 Catherine M. Vitetta
ALL RIGHTS RESERVED WORLDWIDE

ISBN: 978-1-951280-37-6

Unless otherwise noted, Scriptures are taken from the KING JAMES VERSION®. Public Domain.

Cover Design: Don Patton, Image Credit: Freepik

DEDICATION & ACKNOWLEDGEMENTS

I would like to dedicate this book to its "ghost writer" - the Holy Spirit of the living God!

I found it quite amusing that the Lord would have me write a devotional because honestly, I have never even read a devotional. I have always read the Bible as my devotional material, in order to learn of God directly through His Holy Word. I truly feel that as I wrote this book, I was only a scribe for the Holy Spirit and a willing vessel for the Lord.

The Lord never ceases to amaze me in the myriad of unexpected ways in which He chooses to utilize His willing children for His Kingdom purposes. Although many times we feel that we lack the skills to do what the Lord has personally called us to do, we must always remember Matthew 19:26 which states "WITH God, ALL things are possible," especially when we keep our eyes on Jesus! We serve an amazing God!

I would also like to thank my dear friends and siblings in Christ, Pastor Tom and Marcia Patterson, for their friendship, mentorship, prayers, wisdom, guidance, and assistance in helping me to complete this assignment for the Lord. They truly have a servant's heart!

Finally, I would like to thank Manifest International for their prayer filled, Holy Spirit led guidance in the process of the final work necessary for the completion and production of this book for the Lord. I truly believe it was a "match made in Heaven."

CONTENTS

i	Introduction	1
Ch 1	The Church at Ephesus	7
Ch 2	The Church at Smyrna	23
Ch 3	The Church at Pergamum	37
Ch 4	The Church at Thyatira	49
Ch 5	The Church at Sardis	59
Ch 6	The Church at Philadelphia	67
Ch 7	The Church at Laodicea	77
	Final Reflections	95
	A Call to the Romans Road	97

Introduction

Our Lord and Savior, Jesus, desires to draw all of us into a deeper understanding of His heart and into a deeper relationship with Him. If you are reading this right now, I want to assure you that it is not by accident. The Master Potter, our sovereign Lord, is seeking you out at this time to fashion you into ALL that He has designed for you to become in order to fulfill His Kingdom purposes here on planet Earth.

As you will see, the Lord will reference His letters to the seven churches in the Book of Revelation as the framework upon which we will learn more about what is in the heart of Jesus, what pleases Him, and what displeases Him. We will unpack these scriptures one at a time beginning with some Biblical history. These letters to the seven churches in Asia were written by the Apostle John while he was banished to the island of Patmos as punishment for preaching the gospel. He received these words directly from our Lord and Savior, Jesus. We must keep in mind that these letters written by the Lord through his servant John were specifically intended for the church. It was not intended for the unbelievers. The Lord's intention was to provide encouragement as well as correction for His followers. It was the Lord's desire that the seven churches shine their light in an otherwise spiritually dark world.

I find it very interesting that God chose to utilize a small portion of scripture from the Book of Revelation to provide to all of us a deeper revelation of His heart and what He would like to see from us, His children. In the past, I hurriedly skipped over these particular passages because I was so eager to read about the end-times events which will precede the return of Jesus, some of which are still yet to come in this world.

Like me, you may now be thinking, "Well, what does this have to do with me today?" I believe that one of the most important goals of the Lord for writing this book is to prepare His church for His return in ways that are far more important than preservation of our physical body. His goal is to ensure that His church is prepared spiritually and emotionally to endure the anticipated end time events.

Many of us who await the Lord's return with joyful anticipation have done some preparing in practical ways for the events to come. Some of us have stored up food and water for the time of lack ahead, others have been led to physically move to another area, others have started small home churches, etc. It is one thing to do these things in obedience to how the Lord leads us specifically, but another thing altogether to do these tasks out of fear for what may lie ahead. We must each be led by the Lord, and not by our fear or our flesh.

With this said, if we are not right with God spiritually, and we are not emotionally prepared to serve Him with all that is in us, no matter what happens in world events in the days to come, what difference does food, shelter, and short-term physical survival make? After all, as Mark 8:3 states, "For what shall it profit a man, if he shall gain the whole world, and lose his own soul?"

Therefore, these passages are actually a very timely word from the Lord for believers living today. The Lord continues to speak to all of us through His Holy Word in the Bible. I believe the Lord is asking us as His children to examine ourselves in order to ensure that we are all fully ready for His return. His deepest desire is to spend all eternity with us! We don't want to miss it!

You see, the Lord already expressed His intense love for us through His actions: His humble birth, life, horrific death, and resurrection from the dead to free His creation from the bondages of sin and death! Rather, this book is about what the Lord longs to receive back from His beloved creation! As followers of Christ Jesus, it is our job to learn of Him, worship Him, serve Him, and obey Him. These words can cause a carnal person to *shudder*. However, for those of us who love the Lord, the funny thing is that the level of personal joy we experience when we follow, learn, worship, serve, and obey Him is incredible and hard to put into words! It is our job to always remain open to the promptings of the Holy Spirit and follow as He leads us.

The Lord's perspective is always the eternal, not the temporal. It is His greatest desire that ALL of His children spend eternity with Him in paradise! John 6:39 states, "And this is the Father's will which hath sent Me, that all which He hath given Me I should lose nothing but should raise it up again at the last day." It is important to know the Lord's heart and desires, and what pleases and displeases Him, so that we can repent of any wrongdoing and act upon that which is pleasing to the Lord. In other words, we need to be fully ready at all times to meet our Lord and Savior. We know not the day or the hour when we will finally meet Him face to face.

As I was pondering how we do not know the day or hour of the Lord's return, the parable of the Ten Virgins in Matthew 25 came to mind. As I thought about this parable, I realized something that had never occurred to me before. All ten virgins believed in their bridegroom, all were awaiting His return, and all were prepared to varying degrees to meet him upon His arrival. This is how all current followers of Christ are the same as the ten virgins: we believe in our Bridegroom, we await our Bridegroom's return, and we are all ready to meet our Bridegroom in varying degrees of preparation. It is that last clause *in varying degrees* that needs to be more closely investigated.

In the story of the ten virgins, all of them had oil in their lamps initially, but only five of them kept the oil levels full, and had additional oil on hand just in case it was needed in preparation to meet their bridegroom. These were the five wise virgins who later went on to the wedding supper with their groom. The five foolish virgins were slothful in that they did not bother to plan ahead and bring extra oil for their lamps. When the bridegroom approached, the foolish virgins found that they had run out of oil and were actually not ready for their bridegroom's arrival. Because the foolish virgins were not ready to meet the bridegroom when he arrived, they were not allowed into the wedding supper. Their bridegroom said to them in Matthew 25:12, "Verily I say unto you, I know you not."

Please let that sink in! These were fellow believers who did not make it into the wedding supper because they became slothful and were not, in fact, prepared for their bridegroom's arrival! Please don't let that be you! The Lord wants to share His heart with you to ensure you remain or become a wise virgin. Our actions and the motivations thereof will determine our eternal destination – heaven with the Lord or hell without Him.

Are you truly ready for the Lord's return?

As we go through these passages of Revelation, we will also stop to ponder what this means in our lives today. Questions for reflection are posed throughout the book so that we invite the Word of God into our hearts to help us prepare and be ready for the Lord's return. As you consider your answers to these questions, please be honest with yourself. The Lord already knows your answers and He already knows the truth about you. Now, He wants YOU to know the truth about you so you can be led by His Spirit into making wiser decisions and choices.

My prayer for you is that the Lord uses this book to touch your heart in such a way so as to ensure that you remain ready for His return and so that you can spend all eternity with Him! As you use this book to examine yourselves through the lens of His eyes and His heart, may the Lord Jesus richly bless you. Amen.

CHAPTER ONE
The Church at Ephesus

Revelation 2:1-7 - 1 Unto the angel of the church of Ephesus write; These things saith he that holdeth the seven stars in his right hand, who walketh in the midst of the seven golden candlesticks; 2 I know thy works, and thy labour, and thy patience, and how thou canst not bear them which are evil: and thou hast tried them which say they are apostles, and are not, and hast found them liars: 3 And hast borne, and hast patience, and for my name's sake hast laboured, and hast not fainted. 4 Nevertheless I have [somewhat] against thee, because thou hast left thy first love. 5 Remember therefore from whence thou art fallen, and repent, and do the first works; or else I will come unto thee quickly, and will remove thy candlestick out of his place, except thou repent. 6 But this thou hast, that thou hatest the deeds of the Nicolaitans, which I also hate. 7 He that hath an ear, let him hear what the Spirit saith unto the churches; To him that overcometh will I give to eat of the tree of life, which is in the midst of the paradise of God.

The very first letter was written to the church at Ephesus, which happened to be a coastal city in what is now Turkey. Of all the seven churches, the church at Ephesus was the closest to Patmos. Ephesus was a major city at the crossroads of Greek and Oriental cultures and so, Ephesian people participated in idolatry of false gods and goddesses, such as Diana – the goddess of fertility. Ephesians were also immersed in magical arts. Therefore, since these false religions flourished in this area at this time in history, the true Church at Ephesus suffered much persecution.

Also of note, is that every letter is addressed to the angel of each church. In both the Greek and Hebrew languages, angel refers to a "messenger," which actually refers to the church leaders. Following His address to the church leaders, Jesus begins by identifying an aspect of Himself so that there is no question in the recipient's mind who is addressing them. In His letter to Ephesus, which is quoted above, Jesus states He is the one holding the seven stars in His right hand, and the one who walks in the midst of the seven candlesticks. Revelation 1:20 had stated that the seven stars are the angels of the seven churches, while the seven candlesticks represent the seven churches. In other words, Jesus is the ultimate head and overseer of the true church. He is God!

Jesus then continues his letter to the Church of Ephesus by commending them on their diligent work, patience in suffering, and firm stance against evil. In the face of great opposition and persecution, the Christians in Ephesus held strong to their beliefs in the gospel message. They did not compromise their beliefs to gain acceptance or popularity in the general population at Ephesus, and they willingly suffered in the natural because of their firm stance. The Lord commended them for this.

It is clear that the Lord expects His children to stand steadfast and true in their faith, and to speak the truth in love. He commends those who suffer for His namesake, and for righteousness. How do we know this? Because the Word of God in the Bible says so! Some examples are:

Matthew 10:33 - 33 [Jesus speaking] But whosoever shall deny me before men, him will I also deny before my Father which is in heaven.

1 Peter 3:14-15 - 14 But and if ye suffer for righteousness' sake, happy [are ye]: and be not afraid of their terror, neither be troubled; 15 But sanctify the Lord God in your hearts: and [be] ready always to [give] an answer to every man that asketh you a reason of the hope that is in you with meekness [gentleness] and fear [respect.]

Again, the Lord wants us to present and defend the full truth of the gospel message in a kind, gentle, and respectful manner.

> **QUESTION**: Do I compromise my statement of faith and beliefs in order to gain acceptance or avoid confrontation? Do I only present partial Biblical truths instead of the full truth? Do I keep my faith to myself so that I do not have to defend my beliefs to anyone?

_____

_____

_____

_____

_____

_____

_____

_____

_____

Next, we understand that the Church of Ephesus did not tolerate evildoers or false teachers. Their love of the truth motivated them to test those who claimed to be Christians to see if they were the "real deal" so to speak. This, too, Jesus commended.

We currently live in a time where many false doctrines are being preached. Sadly, there are people who intentionally seek out these churches that teach them what they want to hear rather than the truth.

2 Timothy 4: 1-4 states, "I charge thee therefore before God, and the Lord Jesus Christ, who shall judge the quick and the dead at His appearing and His Kingdom; Preach the word; be instant in season, and out of season; reprove, rebuke, exhort with all longsuffering and doctrine. For the time will come when they will not endure sound doctrine; but after their own lusts shall they heap to themselves teachers, having itching ears; and they shall turn away their ears from the truth, and shall be turned into fables."

The Word of God instructs us to always be at the ready to preach the truth of the gospel message. We are to firmly rebuke false doctrines and are to patiently teach and comfort those who do not know the truth. The Bible warns that there will come a time when people will actually seek out these false doctrines if it justifies their lusts and sin.

We must always remember that no one is guaranteed tomorrow! Once a person leaves this Earth, their eternal destiny will be set after they are judged by the one true God. While we are still living and breathing, we still have the opportunity to decide to fully follow Jesus and keep the oil in our lamps full. This knowledge should compel a true Christian into action!

> **QUESTION**: Do I verify what has been taught to me by comparing it to the Word of God in the Holy Bible? Or do I just open my head and let whatever information we are given fall in? Or do I just pretend to be listening intently to a teaching while I am really only day-

dreaming or planning my next activity after church?

_____
_____
_____
_____
_____
_____
_____
_____
_____
_____
_____

There's a saying that goes, "I can sit in a garage all day long and say 'beep-beep,' – but that does not make me a car!" In a similar manner, just because I go to church and attend Bible studies does not make me a Christian. Think about that for a moment. How many people do you know who claim to be Christians yet continue to live worldly, sinful, self-centered lives?

Whenever we hear a teaching, we must be prepared to ask, "What does the Bible have to say about this?" We must ask this regardless of how much we like or do not like the speaker delivering the message or the message itself.

> *Lamentations 3:40 NASB95 - 40 Let us examine and probe our ways, And let us return to the LORD.*
>
> *2 Corinthians 13:5 - 5 Examine yourselves, whether ye be in the faith; prove your own selves. Know ye not your own selves, how that Jesus Christ is in you, except ye be reprobates?*

These scriptures are saying that we need to think critically about our lives and our walk with the Lord.

> *Psalm 139:23-24 - 23 Search me, O God, and know my heart: try me, and know my thoughts: 24 And see if [there be any] wicked way in me, and lead me in the way everlasting.*

In Psalm 139 above, the psalmist is asking the Lord to show him any sin or shortcomings so they can be corrected, in order to restore his good standing and relationship with God. This is good advice for all believers in Christ to follow!

> **QUESTION**: Have I ever asked the Lord to circumcise my heart, meaning to remove and cut off anything and everything He finds displeasing? If yes, what was the end result? If no, why not?

_____

_____

_____

_____

_____

_____

_____

_____

One question I am often asked is, "How can I know for sure if I am born again and truly belong to Christ?"

Romans 10: 9-11 says, "That if thou shalt confess with thy mouth the Lord Jesus, and shalt believe in thine heart that God hath raised Him from the dead, thou shalt be saved. For with the heart man believeth unto righteousness; and with the mouth confession is made unto salvation."

Matthew 7:15-20 says, "You will know them by their fruits." According to Galatians 5:22-23, the fruits of the Spirit are love, joy, peace, patience, kindness, generosity, faithfulness, gentleness, and self-control.

These fruits or qualities develop as a result of you submitting to the work of the Holy Spirit, who now dwells within you. As a born-again follower of Christ, you will never desire to knowingly, habitually, and without remorse continue in sin. Our lives become more and more about our love of God, our obedience to God, and our love for our fellow man. All of this results in our hearts and our lives being changed!

2 Corinthians 5:17 states, "Therefore, if any man be in Christ, he is a new creature: old things are passed away; behold, all things are become new."

> **QUESTION:** Is the Holy Spirit living within me so that I am truly "born again?" What fruits of the Spirit do I have and display? Do those around me see these same qualities in me?

_____

_____

_____

_____

_____

_____

_____

QUESTION: Have I changed since I began my new walk with the Lord? If yes, how have I changed? Do those around me notice these changes?

_____
_____
_____
_____
_____
_____
_____
_____
_____
_____

Jesus said in John 14:15 that "If you love me, you will obey me." A wise pastor friend of mine once said regarding these issues, "God is creator. God is King. God makes the rules in His Kingdom. His followers do not have voting rights." I would like to add that an everlasting, omniscient God has no need of my lowly opinions. Simply put, He is God, and I am not.

The Ten Commandments are entry level commands from God's Law. Do we really adhere to ALL of them? Do you lie? This can include lying by omission which is intentional deception. What about fornication? Fornication is defined as sexual intimacy outside of the Biblical definition of marriage which is between one man and one woman. Even though society is currently trying to redefine marriage, God's view of marriage has not changed.

Both Malachi 3:6 and Hebrews 13:8 declare that God is the same yesterday, today, and forever! This means that God's opinions do not change simply because the opinion of an individual or the opinions of society have changed.

QUESTION: In what ways am I disobedient to the Word of God? Do I love the Lord enough to place him first in my life, deny myself, pick up my cross and follow him in full obedience? If not, what is it that I am clinging onto that the Lord would have me repent of or let go of? Whatever it is, is it worth sealing my eternal fate apart from the Lord in hell?

_____

_____

_____

_____

_____

_____

_____

_____

_____

In the next verse in our Revelation passage to the Ephesians, Jesus explains something else He has against the church at Ephesus. These followers had lost their first love. What did Jesus mean by this? Although the church at Ephesus had retained their devotion to Biblical truths and the gospel message, they had lost their devotion to the Lord himself. Their initial love for God was replaced by religious rules and regulations. How many of the current day churches are guilty of this same offense to the Lord?

This can be compared to an earthly marital relationship. It feels wonderful when our spouse does things out of their love for us. It feels awful when these marital tasks are executed out of a sense of compulsion or duty. The Lord wants and deserves our whole heart and devotion! Our obedience and service to God should be grounded in a deep love and reverential respect for Him.

QUESTION: Am I still *in love* with the Lord, or am I just going through the motions? Since all relationships take effort to maintain and/or improve, what can I do to restore that initial deep love I once had for the Lord in the beginning of our relationship?

_____

_____

_____

_____

_____

_____

_____

The last portion of this passage calls the believers at Ephesus to repent of their transgressions. Repent means to "turn away from" and "stop doing" that which is offensive to the Lord. It is so much more than an empty apology. Thankfully, when we truly repent of sin, the Lord is quick to forgive us! How can a loving God who is also a perfect judge forgive us our sins if we never stop participating in them? Wouldn't our intentional continuation in known sin be our statement to God that we love the sin more than we love Him, which is idolatry? And idolatry is sin!

QUESTION: Are there any sins or areas of disobedience to the Lord of which I have not fully repented? Why have I not fully repented? Have I earnestly asked the Lord to help me to fully repent? Have I asked for prayer and support from brothers and sisters in Christ?

_____
_____
_____
_____
_____
_____
_____
_____

Our level of commitment to being fully, 100% obedient to Christ is indicative of our seriousness to follow Him.

> **QUESTION**: Am I completely committed to following my Lord and Savior, Jesus?

_____
_____
_____
_____
_____
_____
_____
_____

I find the next portion of this passage to the Ephesians to be very interesting. Jesus states that if the followers in Ephesus do not repent and resume their former correct ways, He will remove their lampstand from its place.

What is this really saying? Jesus admits that the church at Ephesus started out as righteous followers who were heaven bound. He is telling them that if they do not repent, they will no longer be righteous before Him. He warns them that if they do not repent, He will remove their lampstand and they will no longer be heaven bound. Ouch! I believe this is one of several scriptures that make clear that the doctrine of "once saved, always saved" is a false doctrine. It is very clear from this passage that the church at Ephesus was once righteous, but now is not, and is at risk for being discarded. This is a very sobering message from the Lord!

I am reminded again of the five foolish virgins. Why did they become slothful? They knew they were engaged to their bridegroom, and he was returning for them at an unknown time. Perhaps, they became overconfident. Perhaps, they grew tired waiting for His return. Perhaps, they thought that they could ride the coattails of the five wise virgins and coast into the wedding feast. Like the "once saved, always saved" doctrine implies, they may have believed that it was a "done deal" and they no longer had to put forth their full effort or could now do as they chose without consequence. This is the true danger of this doctrine, as it is contrary to the Lord's instruction to us to continually remain awake and alert for Him at all times.

> *Mark 13:31-37 - 31 [Jesus speaking] Heaven and earth shall pass away: but my words shall not pass away. 32 But of that day and [that] hour knoweth no man, no, not the angels which are in heaven, neither the Son, but the Father. 33 Take ye heed, watch and pray: for ye know not when the time is. 34 For the Son of man is as a man taking a far journey, who left his house, and gave authority to his servants, and to every man his work, and commanded the porter to watch. 35 Watch ye therefore: for ye know*

not when the master of the house cometh, at even, or at midnight, or at the cockcrowing, or in the morning: 36 Lest coming suddenly he find you sleeping. 37 And what I say unto you I say unto all, Watch.

We must continually examine ourselves and repent of any unrighteousness in our lives as we do not know the day or hour we will meet the Lord face to face.

> **QUESTION**: Am I more like a wise virgin or a foolish virgin? Have I been slothful in my faith or devotion? Have I believed wrong things which led me into spiritual complacency?

_____

_____

_____

_____

_____

_____

_____

_____

At the end of this passage to the Ephesians, the Lord states that to him that overcomes, He will grant to eat from the tree of eternal life which is in Paradise with God. Again, one must overcome the flesh and sin in order to receive eternal life with God, and this can only be accomplished with the Holy Spirit. I am thankful to the Lord for showing us the way…His way!

MORE REFLECTIONS ON CHAPTER ONE

CHAPTER TWO
The Church at Smyrna

Revelation 2:8-11 - 8 And unto the angel of the church in Smyrna write; These things saith the first and the last, which was dead, and is alive; 9 I know thy works, and tribulation, and poverty, (but thou art rich) and [I know] the blasphemy of them which say they are Jews, and are not, but [are] the synagogue of Satan. 10 Fear none of those things which thou shalt suffer: behold, the devil shall cast [some] of you into prison, that ye may be tried; and ye shall have tribulation ten days: be thou faithful unto death, and I will give thee a crown of life. 11 He that hath an ear, let him hear what the Spirit saith unto the churches; He that overcometh shall not be hurt of the second death.

Historically, the city of Smyrna ceased to exist from the seventh to the third century B.C. At the end of this time period, the city of Smyrna became an ally of Rome and was resurrected, so to speak, from the dead.

To the church at Smyrna, Jesus identifies himself as the source from which this message came. He is the first and the last which identifies that He is God. The portion which says that He was dead and now is alive denotes His crucifixion and resurrection from the dead. Only Jesus did this for us. This reference to Jesus as well as Smyrna being resurrected from the dead would have provided the intensely persecuted church at Smyrna a great deal of encouragement. It was a clear message from the Lord Himself that even martyrdom for the name of Jesus could not end their lives!

It is interesting to note that Jesus did not criticize the church of Smyrna at all in this letter. He acknowledges that they were suffering greatly for His namesake in real ways that deeply impacted their lives.

Some might ask, why didn't God, who is supposed to BE love and love His creation so very much, deliver the faithful church of Smyrna from their oppressors? This is a loaded question!

First and foremost, I would ask a counter question at this point: How is a diamond produced from a lump of coal in the ground? It is transformed through tons and tons of pressure! Think about that!

I know four women who suffered greatly with drug addiction. Some became homeless on the streets, some resorted to prostitution and stealing to purchase more drugs, some found themselves in the hospital fighting for their lives, and some found themselves in jail for a time. They all experienced rejection from family and friends, as well as an eradication of their self-esteem. They all truly hit "rock bottom." However, each of these ladies would tell you now that it was when they hit "rock bottom" that they were introduced to Jesus. They had a choice to make!

These women chose wisely and are now Spirit-filled believers with awesome ministries for the Lord! Each of them now ministers to other women who find themselves in similar situations. Because these four women experienced victory in their lives through Christ, who better for the Lord to use to give these other women hope that they, too, can have victory through Christ? Only Jesus can turn our misery into a ministry, and transform us from a lump of coal into a diamond for Him!

> **QUESTION**: What are some instances in your life where you prayed to the Lord to deliver you out of a serious and uncomfortable situation, yet you did not see the hoped for results? How did this make you feel?

_____

_____

_____

_____

_____

_____

_____

_____

I know that this can be a very painful question to think about. I believe everyone of us has some stories to tell where we may have felt like the Lord abandoned us in our time of greatest need. There are some scriptures I would like to share regarding this issue.

2 Corinthians 5:7 - 7 For we walk by faith, not by sight.

The "we" are the righteous followers of Christ, and faith is intangible while sight is the tangible things that we see, touch, hear, and feel.

> *Deuteronomy 31:8 NIV - 8 The LORD himself goes before you and will be with you; he will never leave you nor forsake you. Do not be afraid; do not be discouraged."*
>
> *Romans 8:28 - 28 And we know that all things work together for good to them that love God, to them who are the called according to [his] purpose.*

If you follow Christ and believe that all things written in the Bible are from God and are true, then you know that the Lord has never and will never leave us nor forsake us, even if our emotions tell us otherwise. Emotions can be very strong, but they are also fleeting. As followers of Christ, we need to intentionally purpose in our hearts to listen to the Holy Spirit and not our feelings. And, yes, I know this can be a challenge during times of heightened emotions. It can truly be an immense struggle.

Some might ask, "Why does God allow the struggle?" The answer may lie in the story of how a mere caterpillar transforms into a beautiful butterfly. As you know, the caterpillar wraps itself tightly in a cocoon, much like our more serious challenges here on earth can bind us up also. Once the caterpillar has changed into a butterfly, it has to free itself from the cocoon. This newly formed butterfly is stuffed in this strong cocoon barely able to move, let alone fight its way out with a newly formed and unfamiliar body.

Those of us with "softer hearts" may want so much to help that baby butterfly! However, what would happen if we came along, interrupted God's perfect plan for that butterfly, and carefully cracked open that tough cocoon to free the butterfly from that difficult situation? Do you realize that the butterfly would not be able to fly and would soon die? In fact, it is the difficult struggle to free itself from the cocoon that builds its muscles and makes it strong enough to fly and become what God always meant for it to be!

Similarly, God uses our spiritual struggles against our flesh and emotions to strengthen our spiritual muscles so that we can become what He wants us to be, which is pure and holy people who are ready for His return. If we allow the Lord to complete the work in us that He has started through a particular circumstance, we can emerge stronger spiritually, emotionally, and even physically. Our faith and trust in the Lord can grow stronger, and our relationship with the Lord can grow deeper. In persevering with a good attitude and trust in the Lord, we can bring glory to Him. As the people around us watch our Godly responses to challenging circumstances, we may be planting seeds that could bring them closer to the Lord.

For example, I suffered the recent, unexpected loss of my husband who also happened to be a very strong pastor for the Lord. I had no idea how my behavior and words deeply affected those around me during this time. Without going into great detail, I later learned that a non-believing family member said to another, "Huh? Maybe there is something to this *Jesus thing* after all!" That was one of the many gifts the Lord allowed me to see as I meandered through the grief process in the best way that I knew how, which was with the Lord right by my side the entire time!

> **QUESTION**: Can I identify some of the positive results that emerged following that situation from which the Lord did not deliver me?
>
> _____
>
> _____
>
> _____
>
> _____

_____

_____

_____

_____

_____

If adequate time has passed since you faced a difficult situation or challenge, it will be easier for you to see the positive results that God worked out of it. It is my hope and prayer that you can now begin to see the good that can result from something considered bad in and of itself in the natural.

Here are some scriptures that address the answer to the above question in a more general sense:

> *1 Peter 5:10 NIV - 10 And the God of all grace, who called you to his eternal glory in Christ, after you have suffered a little while, will himself restore you and make you strong, firm and steadfast.*

> *James 1:12 NIV - 12 Blessed is the one who perseveres under trial because, having stood the test, that person will receive the crown of life that the Lord has promised to those who love him.*

Life challenges can either bring out the best in us or the worst in us, and that choice is ours to make. When we stand intentionally firm and true to our commitment to fully follow Christ, it will be evident during the trials of life. It is easy to profess to love and follow the Lord when our lives are going just as we would like them to, but it is much more of a challenge to remain steadfast in the Lord when our lives are falling apart.

Let's look at the life of Job. Job was a man who loved and obeyed God and was righteous before Him. Job's life was going great by our human standards. He had a loving wife, many children, and was very prosperous in the natural. Satan saw this and challenged God by saying that Job was faithful to God only because God had blessed him! To prove Satan wrong, God allowed Satan to destroy everything in Job's life with the exception that he could not kill Job.

Immediately, Satan killed off Job's livestock (which were his livelihood,) killed his servants, and then killed all of his children. What did Job do after all of this? Did he question God or curse God? He did neither. Instead, he put on his mourning clothes and worshipped God. Job's attitude was that he came into this world with nothing, and he will leave this world with nothing, and he will continue to bless the name of the Lord regardless of his circumstances. Job's faithfulness to God in the face of unimaginable and total loss gave immense glory to God!

> **QUESTION**: Have I been, or am I, able to worship, pray to, and remain obedient to the Lord during times of challenge or loss? In what situations was I able to do so and give glory to the Lord? In what situations was I not able to do so, and have I repented of this before the Lord?

_____

_____

_____

_____

_____

_____

_____

_____

Today's false prosperity doctrine treats our Lord and Savior like a cosmic vending machine. Many seemingly come to the Lord only after they are promised earthly riches as a result of following a "God of love who wants only to bless His children." Those who do happen to be blessed with earthly riches only continue to beg God for more and more. Those who do not receive the earthly treasure they desire, wind up walking away from the Lord in due time, saying that Christianity did not work for them. Either way, this scenario is so sad, disgusting, and extremely disrespectful of our Lord Jesus who suffered greatly, died, and rose from the dead to allow each and every one of us the opportunity to be reconciled to God and spend all eternity with Him. THAT is the true treasure the Lord promises us when we overcome the flesh and sin!

Each person on this earth will experience good times as well as bad. That is just how life is! However, in His letter to Smyrna, Jesus is actually referring to the future intense persecution of some of His followers there which would involve incarceration, physical suffering, and possible death simply because of their steadfast and firm belief in Him. In the Lord's abundant mercy, He gave them warning of what was to befall them so they could prepare themselves spiritually, emotionally, and physically to endure the test. Jesus, also, promises great Heavenly rewards and eternal life with Him to those who remain strong and true to Him.

> *Matthew 10:28 - 28 And fear not them which kill the body, but are not able to kill the soul: but rather fear him which is able to destroy both soul and body in hell.*

Now, let's look at Jesus' first Apostles in the New Testament. The original Apostles were Jesus' choicest followers. They were in His inner circle and were His most trusted confidants on this earth. Yet, at the time of Jesus' crucifixion, Mark 14:50 states, "that they all forsook Him and fled" out of fear for their lives. But after the resurrection, they boldly proclaimed the gospel and did not back down. The trial of their faith, and even their failure, had made them stronger. They would not make the same mistake again.

Every one of the Lord's Apostles suffered intense persecution for preaching the gospel message. Every one of them, except for John, died a martyr's death for their profession of faith in Jesus. It is important to remember that there is absolutely nobody on this earth who would intentionally suffer and die for a lie!

Why would we who live in this world today and follow the Lord Jesus expect to be treated any differently than the original Apostles? Certainly, we cannot believe that we are any better or more special than they. The Bible says in Romans 2:11, "For there is no respecter of persons with God," which means that He does not play favorites. We must be ready because as we grow closer each day to the return of Jesus, persecution of the Christians will grow more and more intense on a global basis against anyone and everyone who is a follower of Jesus.

Just as with the church of Smyrna, Jesus has warned that His end time church will suffer intense persecution prior to His return. In Luke 21: 12 when Jesus is speaking about end time events, He states, "But before all these [events], they shall lay their hands upon you, and persecute you, delivering you up to the synagogues, and into prisons, being brought before kings and rulers for my name's sake." Again, in His abundant mercy, He gives those of us today warning so we can be prepared.

> **QUESTION**: Am I prepared spiritually, emotionally, and physically to stand firm and steadfast in my faith and trust in Jesus even unto death as the original Apostles and church of Smyrna once did?

_____

_____

_____

_____

QUESTION: What can I do to get myself ready to stand steadfast in Jesus in the face of death? Do I even want to remain steadfast in Jesus in the face of death?

In writing these questions that the Lord has posed through me, I pondered what my own response would be. I have to admit that I found it to be challenging. After some research and prayer, I discovered the following which may be of help:

1. We are to live our lives guided by the Holy Spirit, not our flesh.
2. We are to remain "on fire" for the Lord.
3. We are to diligently and continuously seek the truth.

Galatians 5: 16, 24-25 states, "This I say then, walk in the Spirit, and ye shall not fulfill the lusts of the flesh... And they that are Christ's have crucified the flesh with the affections and lusts. If we live in the Spirit, let us also walk in the Spirit."

The best way to walk in the Spirit is to read and know the Word of God in the Bible, and to prayerfully consider what our actions and choices are to be. We will have an inner peace when we are making the choices that are consistent with what the Lord would have us choose and do. When in doubt, we need to seek counsel from a trusted Spirit-filled believer in Christ for prayer and confirmation.

What does it mean to remain "on fire" for the Lord? Leviticus 6:12 states, "And the fire upon the altar shall be burning in it; it shall not be put out: and the priest shall burn wood on it every morning and lay the burnt offering in order upon it; and he shall burn thereon the fat of the peace offerings." For us today, the fire represents our love for Christ. We are now a royal priesthood. The daily sacrifice is our lives now that we place the will of the Lord before our own will and desires. It is the fat that gives meat its rich flavor. When we give our very best and our all to the Lord, it is akin to burning the fat in Old Testament times.

I am reminded again of the story of the ten virgins. The oil in their lamps actually represents the infilling of the Holy Spirit. The five wise virgins kept their lamps full of oil, plus had extra oil. In other words, they kept their full focus on their bridegroom to come. The five foolish virgins eventually ran out of oil because they did not plan ahead. Their focus was divided between their bridegroom and other things such as the cares of this world. When the bridegroom arrived, he found only the wise virgins who kept their lamps filled to the top were satisfactory to become his bride. The foolish virgins who allowed their previously full lamps to run empty were rejected.

We must keep our lamps full of oil at all times. How do we do this? We do this by daily prayer and worship, daily reading and studying the Bible, and by regular fellowship with true Spirit-filled believers in Christ. Fellowship includes church services, Bible studies, as well as social gatherings that are Christ centered. This will also support our efforts to continuously seek the truth.

Finally, in this passage to the believers at Smyrna, the Lord assures His faithful followers that while remaining steadfast in their love and obedience to the Lord through their suffering, they are rich in that they are storing up for themselves treasure in heaven. The Lord promises them eternal life with Him as their reward! And for those of us who may suffer this type of extreme persecution in end-times, this promise from the Lord remains true for us too! Praise the Lord!

MORE REFLECTIONS ON CHAPTER TWO

READY FOR THE KING

CHAPTER THREE
The Church at Pergamum

Revelation 2:12-17 - 12 And to the angel of the church in Pergamos write; These things saith he which hath the sharp sword with two edges; 13 I know thy works, and where thou dwellest, [even] where Satan's seat [is]: and thou holdest fast my name, and hast not denied my faith, even in those days wherein Antipas [was] my faithful martyr, who was slain among you, where Satan dwelleth. 14 But I have a few things against thee, because thou hast there them that hold the doctrine of Balaam, who taught Balac to cast a stumblingblock before the children of Israel, to eat things sacrificed unto idols, and to commit fornication. 15 So hast thou also them that hold the doctrine of the Nicolaitans, which thing I hate. 16 Repent; or else I will come unto thee quickly, and will fight against them with the sword of my mouth. 17 He that hath an ear, let him hear what the Spirit saith unto the churches; To him that overcometh will I give to eat of the hidden manna, and will give him a white stone, and in the stone a new name written, which no man knoweth saving he that receiveth [it].

The city of Pergamum was located 60 miles north of Smyrna somewhat inland. Beginning in roughly 133 B.C., Pergamum was the capital of Asia and remained so for about 400 years. Pergamum was considered a wealthy city much like Ephesus and Smyrna. However, the city as a whole rejected the written Word of God and wisdom of Christ.

Pergamum was located where Satan had a stronghold. The people of Pergamum worshipped several false gods including Zeus who was held as the chief Olympian god. Some believe that Pergamum was the seat of Satan because there was built there an altar to Zeus. There were so many false gods continually worshipped there that it made it difficult for the Christians of Pergamum to worship Christ.

To the believers at Pergamum, Jesus begins by identifying Himself as the One who has the sharp sword with two-edges. In the Greek, the sword to which He is referring is a rhomphaian. A rhomphaian was actually a large, broad sword used by the Romans as a weapon of offense intended to separate and slash. This will be the sword utilized by the Lord in His final judgement upon man described in the Book of Revelation.

In Luke 2:34-35, Mary was listening to a prophecy given by Simeon. Simeon predicted that Jesus' ministry will result in a sharp division among the people, even within the people of Israel. This prophecy was in opposition to the Jewish belief at that time which was that the Messiah would bring peace and prosperity to Israel. The intent of this division of the people was and is to reveal each person's heart and sincerity in seeking the one, true God. It was intended to separate the sheep from the goats, or the believers from the unbelievers.

In the Lord's infinite mercy through this devotional, He is giving each reader the opportunity to examine their heart to ensure it is righteous before Him. It is His greatest desire that His creation spends all eternity with Him. Our choice will determine our eternal destination: the sheep with the Lord or the goats in eternal damnation without Him.

The Lord then commends the church of Pergamum for holding steadfast to their faith in Christ and their faith in the truth of the gospel message while in the midst of continual worship of false gods. They even remained faithful after one of their own was martyred for their profession of faith in Christ!

> **QUESTION**: Have I been in a situation where I had to choose between defending my faith, remaining quiet, or denying my faith in the face of ridicule, opposition, or possible persecution? What did I choose as my response? Why?

_____

_____

_____

_____

_____

_____

_____

_____

I am ashamed to admit that I chose to remain quiet in the face of opposition when I was very young in my walk with the Lord. And I will share with you exactly what the Lord clearly spoke to my heart after this incident: "If you deny me before man, I will deny you before the Father!" (Quoting Matthew 10:33.) The Lord was painfully clear with me how He felt about me not standing steadfast in openly professing and being ready to defend my faith! I repented, of course. The experience changed me.

QUESTION: From my own response to the question above, do I think the Lord approved of my choice? If I think He did not approve, what would have been a better, Biblically correct response? Did I repent?

_____
_____
_____
_____
_____
_____
_____
_____
_____

In the next portion of the Lord's letter to the church of Pergamum, He refers to a story in the Old Testament involving two people named Balaam and Balak. This story occurred just prior to the Israelites entering into the promised land after their exodus from Egypt. Their story is written about in chapters 22-24 in the Book of Numbers in the Bible. In order to understand the points that the Lord is making in this letter, we need to have an understanding of who these people were and what it was they did.

Balak was a King at that time who was against Israel. He paid Baalam, who was a known sorcerer, to put a curse on Israel. Since Baalam was not able to put a curse on Israel, he devised another scheme to hurt Israel. Baalam advised King Balak to encourage the Israelites to commit sexual sin, and to practice idolatry by worshipping pagan gods. Of course, these things are against God's Law for His people.

The letter to the Christians at Pergamum also mentions the

Nicolaitans. Historians do not know much about the practices of the Nicolaitans, so it is a little unclear what the Nicolaitans believed, taught, or practiced that the Lord hated so much. Clearly, they practiced things that were contrary to the Word of God. Some people believe that because the word Nicolaitans is derived from the root words of "ruler" and "people," that they may have been a religious sect that firmly ruled their adherents through strict rules and oppression, rather than the servant-leadership style that Jesus taught. Somehow, the people who held these false beliefs infiltrated the true church at Pergamum. Therefore, the Lord is expressing His displeasure that this has been allowed and tolerated.

> **QUESTION**: Do I attend a church that fully follows the teachings of Jesus and the Bible, or one that has changed their beliefs to conform to the current opinions of society? Have I even looked at what my church is teaching to see if their teachings are fully aligned with the Word of God?

_____

_____

_____

_____

_____

_____

_____

_____

Satan is crafty. He never devises a lie that is completely 100%

untrue. He cleverly mixes a little truth with his lies. But Galatians 5:9 says that "a little leaven leavens the whole batch." In other words, like yeast that works its way into dough for bread, even a slight error, intended or not, perverts the truth and misleads the people.

> *1 Peter 5:8 – 8 Be sober, be vigilant; because your adversary the devil, as a roaring lion, walketh about, seeking whom he may devour:*

This is a very clear warning to God's people. First, it places the responsibility to not be deceived by our enemy on you and me! Yes, WE are responsible for being, or not being, deceived. We must remain sober and clear minded at all times. We must remain diligent.

Remain diligent in what way you might ask?

1. We must read and study the Word of God. Many believe that the Bible is God's love letter to His people. In it contains what the Lord desires to receive back from His human creation, what He finds to be righteous and acceptable, and what He finds to be unrighteous and unacceptable. There are many historical stories as well as parables in the Bible which exemplify the consequences of our righteous behaviors as well as unrighteous behaviors. Through knowledge of God's written Holy Word, we are given every opportunity to choose righteousness and that which is pleasing to our Lord for our eternal salvation.

2. We must thoughtfully and prayerfully select those whom we seek out for counsel, teaching and fellowship. As we grow in our faith and knowledge of the Lord, it is vital that we purpose to spend time with Spirit filled believers who are obedient to the Word of God, whose lives reflect Godliness, who 'walk the talk' and lead by example. These are the ones who live Godly lives which we can emulate, the ones we should listen to for learning purposes, and the ones with whom we should

seek counsel when in doubt or confusion. Again, we must read and study the Word of God in order to be able to identify a true and faithful shepherd of the flock.

3. We must always be watchful for possible enemy attacks. Again, 1 Peter 5:8 warns us that our enemy is always looking for ways to separate us from our Heavenly Father, or at the very least render us ineffective for God's Kingdom purposes. As we grow in head and heart knowledge of the Word of God, we become better able to discern when truth is mixed with lies – which is one of the enemy's primary weapons he utilizes to attempt to manipulate believers into sin.

In His letter to Pergamum, the Lord states that those in His church who are following these false doctrines need to repent and stop, or else He will come and judge them with the sword of His mouth. God will not tolerate false doctrines being taught in His church or immorality of any kind in His people, both of which destroy the church from within.

> **QUESTION**: Can I identify any teachings that I have come across that go against the Word of God in the Bible? Have I even investigated teachings I have heard to determine if they align fully with the Word of God in the Bible?

_____

_____

_____

_____

_____

QUESTION: Is Biblical immorality of any kind tolerated in my church or circle of fellow believers?

QUESTION: If I answered yes to either of the above questions, what do I sense the Lord would have me do about it?

_____

_____

_____

_____

_____

Once again, Jesus concludes His letter with a promise to His people who are obedient overcomers. He uses the example of the overcomer receiving a stone with their name on it. This is a reference to the Roman custom of giving the victors of an athletic competition a white stone with their name on it. This stone served as their "ticket" to enter into the awards celebration later on. Our awards celebration begins when we, as obedient overcomers, arrive in Paradise with the Lord!

More Reflections on Chapter Three

CHAPTER FOUR
The Church at Thyatira

Revelation 2:18-29 – 18 And unto the angel of the church in Thyatira write; These things saith the Son of God, who hath his eyes like unto a flame of fire, and his feet [are] like fine brass; 19 I know thy works, and charity, and service, and faith, and thy patience, and thy works; and the last [to be] more than the first. 20 Notwithstanding I have a few things against thee, because thou sufferest that woman Jezebel, which calleth herself a prophetess, to teach and to seduce my servants to commit fornication, and to eat things sacrificed unto idols. 21 And I gave her space to repent of her fornication; and she repented not. 22 Behold, I will cast her into a bed, and them that commit adultery with her into great tribulation, except they repent of their deeds. 23 And I will kill her children with death; and all the churches shall know that I am he which searcheth the reins and hearts: and I will give unto every one of you according to your works. 24 But unto you I say, and unto the rest in Thyatira, as many as have not this doctrine, and which have not known the depths of Satan, as they speak; I will put upon you none other burden. 25 But that which ye have [already] hold fast till I come. 26 And he that overcometh, and keepeth my works unto the end, to him will I give power over the nations: 27 And he shall rule them with a rod of iron; as the vessels of a potter shall they be broken to shivers: even as I received of my Father. 28 And I will give him the morning star. 29 He that hath an ear, let him hear what the Spirit saith unto the churches.

Thyatira was a wealthy inland city in Asia minor that was known in particular for its dyers trade guild which created colorful dyes and paints.

Interestingly, the name Thyatira means "continual sacrifice." To me, this is symbolic of the state of the Christian church there, as they suffered much persecution. The believers in Thyatira worshipped Jesus, the Son of God, while most of the people in their city worshipped the god of the sun. The wealthy trade unions would hold banquets and serve food and delicacies sacrificed to idols. Any Christian refusal to participate in these feasts would be noticed and only add to their persecution. Their lives of obedience to the Lord on Earth were truly a living sacrifice unto Him.

Jesus begins His letter to the church of Thyatira by directly identifying Himself as the Son of God. In the other letters to the churches, Jesus only described identifying aspects of Himself as opposed to directly identifying Himself. Jesus' choice of words here is interesting to note in that Thyatira's pagan or false god, Apollo, was the son of the chief pagan or false god, Zeus. In light of this, Jesus established His supreme deity as the Son of the one true, living God!

Jesus goes on to describe Himself with eyes like flames of fire which denotes brightness, intensity, and an all-consuming, penetrating nature. Nothing escapes the Lord's notice! He describes His feet like fine, shiny brass which indicates strength, brightness, and majesty. He has just described aspects of Himself to the church of Thyatira which would illustrate to them that He is far more glorious than the false god Apollo.

Jesus begins by commending the church of Thyatira for their good works, love (which was lacking at the church of Ephesus), faith, service, and patient endurance. When we truly love and serve the Lord, we will love others as we love ourselves. In turn, this motivates us to be kind and respectful of others, demonstrate patience towards others, and leads us to cheerfully serve others as needs arise. These works in and of themselves do not save us but will be the result IN us once we are saved by the Lord by His grace through our faith in Him.

> **QUESTION**: In what circumstances do/did I see myself as loving and serving others in a Christ like fashion? Conversely, in which circumstances have I failed to do so with others, and what could I have done differently to show the love of Christ in a better manner in that situation?

_____

_____

_____

_____

_____

_____

_____

_____

You may be asking, "What does this mean to me today?" When many of us begin a serious walk with the Lord, we repent of and stop doing those activities that the Lord deems sinful and displeasing to Him. What often happens is that many of our friends and family do not like the "new" us. Our changed behavior convicts them of their wrongdoing, whether they know it or not. We get accused of thinking that we are now somehow better than they are, and this ultimately results in fewer and fewer social invitations. This is just a small taste of persecution compared to what the earliest Christian believers experienced!

QUESTION: As a Christian, how do I handle rejection from those with whom I was once close? Do I lash out in anger? Do I try to justify and/or soften my new views in front of them? Do I try to partially resume my previous activities so that I can somehow maintain these friendships and my worldly reputation while pursuing my new faith in Jesus more quietly?

_____

_____

_____

_____

_____

_____

_____

_____

All of the above reactions involve compromise. As fleshly beings, we literally want our cake and to eat it too! But the truth of the matter is that we cannot have one foot in the Kingdom of God and one foot in the world.

The Lord gave everything He had to reconcile us back to Him. How can we expect our Lord and Savior to welcome us with open arms while we are still hanging onto our worldly treasures? In my mind, I picture the Lord running to me with both arms reaching forward, while I run to Him with one arm forward and the other dragging along my old boyfriends! Adultery is adultery. We commit spiritual adultery against the Lord whenever we love or value something more than we do Him. You cannot "cheat a little bit" on your spouse. You either cheat or you don't! We are either ALL in for the Lord or we are not. Think about that.

Years ago, I went through 13 years of unsuccessful fertility treatments before I was blessed with my one and only child through adoption. This child became my entire world. As the years went on, sadly my relationship with the Lord was put on the back burner, so to speak. The Lord, in His infinite mercy, actually told me directly during prayer one evening that my child was an idol before Him. I felt like I had been punched in the stomach when I heard those words in my spirit! Deep down, I knew it was true, and I had such remorse that I had done that to my Lord and Savior after all He had done for me on that cross.

> **QUESTION**: Am I willing to give up ALL of my worldly friends and worldly pleasures and treasures for the Lord and His promise of eternal life? Is there something or someone in particular that is holding me back from FULL submission to Christ? What is it?

_____

_____

_____

_____

_____

_____

_____

_____

Anything that you cannot or will not let go of for the Lord is an idol! The Lord wants you to repent and have a right heart before Him. He will help you to truly repent if you earnestly ask Him, as He did for me in my situation. He will circumcise your heart of all

He finds displeasing if you earnestly ask Him, meaning that He will cut it off so that it will no longer hinder your relationship with Him. Again, He does this only if and when you earnestly ask Him to. He will never force it upon you as He never takes away our free will. But please remember, the choices we make on earth determine our eternal destination!

Jesus continues His letter to Thyatira with an admonishment that they tolerate the false prophetess Jezebel. We need to understand who Jezebel was and what she did in order to understand the Lord's message to us. Her story is written about in 1 and 2 Kings in the Bible. Jezebel was a worshipper of Baal who married King Ahab of Israel. She enticed King Ahab to worship Baal instead of the God of Abraham, Isaac, and Jacob. Her pagan religion with its immoral sexual rituals and temple prostitution spread throughout Israel. She also manipulated and schemed behind the scenes to obtain a vineyard desired by her husband. As if that wasn't bad enough, she killed prophets of God to silence them! In other words, Israel was now tolerating worship of false gods, sexual immorality, trickery to obtain what was desired, as well as ridding Israel of the true prophets of the Lord!

Think about this, the church was tolerating outright sin! But isn't this what is being tolerated in the churches of today? How many churches condone and perform same-sex marriages, even though this goes against the Holy Word of God in the Bible? (See Matthew 19:4-6; 1 Corinthians 7:2-5.) How many churches hang their rainbow pride flags and put them on display, even though this promotes sin and stands in the way of true repentance for sinners? (See Psalm 1:1.) How many "preachers" today claim to be Christian and follow Jesus, yet are openly gay? Jesus would never condone such things! There are now even churches that promote drag queens in the pulpit! The list goes on....

Jesus was whipped mercilessly, as He took the beating for our sin. We crucify Him over and over again when we tolerate sin! Yet, He waits with patient endurance to allow us time to repent and forsake our sin. If we refuse to repent of our sin, then Romans 1:18-32 says that the Lord will turn us over to our sin and to a reprobate mind, allowing us to do as we please, and leaving us to suffer the consequences both in the natural as well as in eternity. Please, don't let that be you!

In His letter to Thyatira, Jesus comments that He did give Jezebel time to repent, but she chose not to repent. The Lord always gives us time to repent of sin. However, the time allowed for us to repent will run out. There will be an end to this grace period given by the Lord. Proverbs 29:1 states a warning, "He who is often reproved, yet stiffens his neck, will suddenly be broken beyond healing." Those who remain stubborn over time refusing to submit to the promptings of the Lord will ultimately suffer the Lord's wrath, punishment, and final judgement.

> **QUESTION**: What is it specifically that the Lord wants me to repent of? Is it my intention to repent, or to continue in my sin?

_____

_____

_____

_____

_____

_____

_____

_____

_____

_____

If we need to ponder what it is that we want, whether to repent or not, then we do not have a right heart attitude towards the Lord. Please remember, the Bible says that none of us are guaranteed tomorrow, and we do not know what each day will bring. (See Proverbs 27:1.) The last thing anyone of us should want is to stand before the Lord in judgement after our physical death before we had a chance to repent!! Once we physically die, our eternal destination will be set by what we have done, whether good or bad! At that point, there is no further opportunity for repentance. Our eternal fate is sealed!

In the next portion of this letter to the church of Thyatira, Jesus is stating clearly that severe punishment awaits those who remain unrepentant. Again, our eternal destination is determined by the choices we make while here on Earth. The Bible is clear that those who reject Jesus will be permanently separated from Him in a place of suffering and torment for all eternity.

In His mercy, the Lord encourages His faithful followers in Thyatira to let them know that they will be spared further burdens on this earth because of their faithfulness. He instructs them to hold on and to remain steadfast. He is telling them to continue in growing their faith, their love of Him and others, spreading the gospel, as well as works of service for the benefit of the brethren which are done unto Him. In other words, He is telling them to continue being like the five wise virgins in Matthew 25 until His return at an unknown time.

He also promises eternal rewards to those who honor Him until the end! The five wise virgins went into the wedding supper with their groom as their reward for remaining steadfast and true in their groom's absence. In His letter to Thyatira, the Lord promises His steadfast servants authority to rule and reign with Him in the world to come on the Earth once He has vanquished the darkness! Once that happens, only the beautiful light of Christ will remain!

More Reflections on Chapter Four

CHAPTER FIVE
The Church at Sardis

Revelation 3:1-6 – 1 And unto the angel of the church in Sardis write; These things saith he that hath the seven Spirits of God, and the seven stars; I know thy works, that thou hast a name that thou livest, and art dead. 2 Be watchful, and strengthen the things which remain, that are ready to die: for I have not found thy works perfect before God. 3 Remember therefore how thou hast received and heard, and hold fast, and repent. If therefore thou shalt not watch, I will come on thee as a thief, and thou shalt not know what hour I will come upon thee. 4 Thou hast a few names even in Sardis which have not defiled their garments; and they shall walk with me in white: for they are worthy. 5 He that overcometh, the same shall be clothed in white raiment; and I will not blot out his name out of the book of life, but I will confess his name before my Father, and before his angels. 6 He that hath an ear, let him hear what the Spirit saith unto the churches.

Sardis was located 50 miles east of Smyrna on top of a 1500-foot-high hill that was only accessible by a very steep path on its south side. This provided the city with a prominent and fortified military advantage. However, Antiochus the Great managed to overcome the city by sending in his military through an unknown crack in the northern wall. In 17 A.D., an earthquake completely destroyed Sardis. After this, the city was rebuilt but never regained the power or influence it had obtained prior to the earthquake. John wrote the letter to Sardis around the year 90 A.D. at the time when the city was still recuperating from this devastating blow.

Jesus begins His letter to Sardis by identifying Himself as God. Many believe that the reference to the seven Spirits of God denotes His omniscience.

Jesus continues speaking to the believers in Sardis by telling them that their reputation indicates that they are alive, but in reality they are dead spiritually. Ouch! It reminds me of something that Jesus said in His encounters with Pharisees, the religious leaders of the Jewish people in Matthew 23:

> *Matthew 23:27-28 – 27 [Jesus speaking] Woe unto you, scribes and Pharisees, hypocrites! For ye are like unto whited sepulchres, which indeed appear beautiful outward, but are within full of dead [men's] bones, and of all uncleanness. 28 Even so ye also outwardly appear righteous unto men, but within ye are full of hypocrisy and iniquity.*

This scripture in Matthew was a harsh insult to the scribes and Pharisees. The inside of a sepulchre (which is an ancient word for tomb) was considered extremely unclean, because anyone who touched a dead body would be considered ceremonially unclean for seven days according to Old Covenant Law. In other words, these people appeared very clean and righteous on the outside, but on the inside they were filled with the highest level of filth. Ouch, again!

Our Lord and Savior is so much more concerned with the condition of our heart than our outward appearance and superficial good deeds. The scribes and Pharisees were more concerned with their outward appearance and the praise of men but were not concerned with what God truly sees which is their heart!

> **QUESTION:** Am I more concerned with my outward appearance and reputation than I am about being righteous before God? If Jesus cracked open my heart right now, what would he find?

_____

_____

_____

_____

_____

_____

_____

_____

At one time, the city of Sardis rested comfortably and confidently on their secure position on top of that hill. Perhaps, they became overconfident and complacent over time. The people of Sardis must have felt that they were immune from military attacks, thus overlooking that crack in their northern wall. It was through that unnoticed crack that their enemy entered, and they met their demise.

In His letter to Sardis, Jesus warns the church of their complacency and warns them to be watchful and to strengthen what they have so as not to lose that too! Because of the history of Sardis, this warning would have been taken very seriously by the believers there.

In a similar manner, we can develop a sense of smug over-confidence when our lives are going as we would like, and we are satisfied with things just the way they are. Sometimes we rest on our past laurels and believe that we can just coast on our current good reputation and situation. We can become quite comfortable with the status quo, which is when we are most likely to become inattentive and lazy, making us ripe for an attack from the enemy.

In the natural, we could look at many marriages today. We are so in love during the early stages of our marriage that all we want to do is please our spouse. As our relationship develops over the years, we can become complacent. It is at this point that many begin to take their spouse for granted and no longer purpose to please them or even pay attention to them. This is when spousal dissatisfaction and anger develop, and many marriages sadly fall apart.

This same type of complacency in our relationship with God, that smug over-confidence when things are going well for us, is an enemy of the church as well as to each of us individually. It lulls us into sleepiness both mentally and spiritually. There is a saying that goes, "A chef is only as good as the last meal that he cooked." Just some food for thought. *(Yes, the pun is intended.)*

> **QUESTION**: Have I become complacent in my walk with Christ, thus taking Him for granted? In what ways? What can I do to counteract my complacency and put the Lord first in my life where He belongs? Am I willing to put forth the effort to do so?

Next in His letter, Jesus challenges the church of Sardis to recapture what they once had in Him and to repent of their complacency. The Lord chastises them for being inattentive to Him and His kingdom purposes. The church of Sardis lost their zeal and reverential fear of the Lord and were essentially taking Him for granted, which resulted in them not completing the tasks assigned to them by the Lord. He then warns them of what will happen if they choose not to repent. He states that He will come upon them like an unwelcome, unexpected thief in the night implying that He will take that which is good from them.

I refer back again to the five foolish virgins. They became slothful, or complacent, and were not allowed into the wedding supper with their prospective groom because of it! Please, don't let that be you.

It is interesting to note that Jesus warns these complacent Christians that, if they do not repent, He will blot their names out of the Book of Life. Think about this for a moment. Their names were currently written in the Book of Life, but the Lord says that He will blot their names out if they do not repent of their sin! Could this be another warning of the falsity of the once saved, always saved doctrine? Could this be the "good" that He will remove if/when He comes as a thief in the night to His lukewarm followers? Praise the Lord for His great mercy, and that there is forgiveness for those who truly repent!

Jesus commends the few righteous believers who remain in Sardis. He states in Revelation 3:4, "Thou hast a few names even in Sardis which have not defiled their garments; and they shall walk with Me in white: for they are worthy." In this passage, the term "garments" is actually referring to the soul. The Hebrews considered the garment of the soul to be holiness, while evil actions or sin put stains on the garment of the soul.

The good news was that there were still a few Christians in Sardis who remained awake, alert, and vigilant for the Lord. Jesus acknowledges this group of obedient Christians who overcame complacency. The white garments that were promised to them represents their righteousness before God, who deems them worthy to spend eternity walking with Him.

The Lord wants His followers to remain on fire for Him, and watchful for Him at all times. Someday, the Lord will return for His people. We are to remain awake, alert, on fire and working for Him in full obedience until that time comes or He calls us home. The eternal reward of spending all eternity with the Lord is THE prize worth fighting for!

MORE REFLECTIONS ON CHAPTER FIVE

CHAPTER SIX

The Church at Philadelphia

Revelation 3:7-13 – 7 And to the angel of the church in Philadelphia write; These things saith he that is holy, he that is true, he that hath the key of David, he that openeth, and no man shutteth; and shutteth, and no man openeth; 8 I know thy works: behold, I have set before thee an open door, and no man can shut it: for thou hast a little strength, and hast kept my word, and hast not denied my name. 9 Behold, I will make them of the synagogue of Satan, which say they are Jews, and are not, but do lie; behold, I will make them to come and worship before thy feet, and to know that I have loved thee. 10 Because thou hast kept the word of my patience, I also will keep thee from the hour of temptation, which shall come upon all the world, to try them that dwell upon the earth. 11 Behold, I come quickly: hold that fast which thou hast, that no man take thy crown. 12 Him that overcometh will I make a pillar in the temple of my God, and he shall go no more out: and I will write upon him the name of my God, and the name of the city of my God, [which is] new Jerusalem, which cometh down out of heaven from my God: and [I will write upon him] my new name. 13 He that hath an ear, let him hear what the Spirit saith unto the churches.

Philadelphia was located southeast of Sardis in an area prone to earthquakes. It was founded by the king of Pergamum in 189 BC. The word Philadelphia is derived from two Greek words meaning "love" and "brothers," and the king named this city in honor of his loyal brother. This city was also known for its wine production and because of this, many of the people of Philadelphia worshipped the god of wine, Dionysius.

Jesus opens this letter as identifying himself as holy and true. He is fully trustworthy and cannot lie as He is holy. Jesus continues adding that He is of a royal lineage, as He is a son of David. He possesses the key of David, is Israel's promised King, and will rule the nations from the throne of Israel someday.

As Philadelphia was a source of much missionary activity throughout Asia, it is believed that the references to the open vs. closed doors refers to the Lord's provision for their unencumbered missionary work. Jesus then commends them for remaining steadfast and true to the gospel message and their calling to evangelize even though they have little strength left.

The synagogue of Satan to which Jesus is referring, denotes those Jews in Philadelphia who were making life hard for the Christians there through intense persecution. Jesus is saying that this sect of Jews were liars and actually belonged to Satan. Jesus then concludes that, ultimately, these non-believers would come to know that Jesus is the Messiah, and every knee will bow before Him – and His true followers!

In today's world, we can see the birth pains prior to the return of Jesus increasing in intensity and frequency. The imagery of birth pains is mentioned in Matthew 24:6-8 which states, "See that you are not alarmed, for this must take place, but the end is not yet. For nation will rise against nation, and Kingdom against Kingdom, and there will be famines and earthquakes in various places. All these are but the beginning of birth pains."

As we keep vigilant watch for the Lord's return, we can see that even in our present time, evil abounds to the point of the world calling that which is evil by Biblical standards good, and that which is good by Biblical standards evil. This is one of the many end time signs mentioned throughout scripture.

Additionally, natural disasters and rumors of war have increased greatly worldwide century by century, continuing to our present time. All of these occurrences would be equivalent to the gradual increase in intensity and frequency of labor pains prior to the birth of a child. Christ's return is our reward, just like holding that new baby is the mother's reward. The new mother is so happy that she no longer remembers the pain of the childbirth as she looks into her newborn's eyes. In a similar manner, scripture tells us in Romans 8:18, "For I reckon the sufferings of the present time are not worthy to be compared to the glory which shall be revealed in us." I cannot fathom the intense joy we will feel standing face to face with our Lord and Savior as He says, "Welcome home!"

But getting back to the growing opposition and the challenges of today's world, many Spirit-filled believers have grown weary in their work for the Lord, even while eagerly awaiting His return.

> **QUESTION**: Have I grown weary in well doing and completing my earthly mission for the Lord? What effect has my weariness had on my walk with and work for the Lord?

_____

_____

_____

_____

_____

_____

I, too, am tired. In addition to the above world-wide issues, I have recently endured a season of intense personal attacks. Our enemy is relentless! But praise the Lord! His Word says in 1 John 4:4, "Greater is He who is in you than the one who is in the world."

You might be wondering about what you can possibly do to combat this battle fatigue in difficult times? I believe the answer lies in the proper care of our physical bodies as well as our spiritual bodies. Since our Spirits are housed in these fleshly bodies, we need to take care of them properly with adequate nutrition, rest, recreation, and medical care. Keeping our bodies in optimal function helps the Spirit of God flow fully in our lives and gives us the natural energy we need to continue on in our work for the Lord.

> **QUESTION**: Am I doing these things to strengthen my physical body? Am I eating healthy, exercising, getting enough rest? What can I improve upon?

Now that we have taken care of these earthly vessels, we can focus on the more important task of fully completing our earthly missions for the Lord. In trying times, we need to be more intensely intentional about keeping our lamps full, like the five wise betrothed brides to be in Matthew 25. We need to set our intentional purpose to do the following daily:

1. Spend time at the Lord's feet and abide in Him, just like Mary in Luke 10:38-42. In this particular story, Jesus came to visit the house of Lazarus, and his sisters Martha and Mary. Martha's focus was on the world around her, in that she remained very busy cooking and cleaning for the Lord, while Mary just sat at the feet of Jesus. Martha complained to Jesus that Mary was not helping her serve all the guests. Jesus' reply was that Mary was to be left alone at His feet as she had chosen the better activity in that moment. This was to stress the importance of spending time with Jesus 'at His feet', so to speak. It does not tell us not to cook and clean for guests, but to consider what needs to be prioritized at any given time.

   QUESTION: When and where can I plan to spend alone time with the Lord at His feet? (This can include prayers spoken out loud or sitting fully silent while waiting upon the Lord for His direction.)

_____

_____

_____

_____

_____

_____

_____

2. Spend time in worship. This is such a beautiful way to enter into the healing and comforting presence of the Lord.

   QUESTION: When and where can I do this? (Worship can be heartfelt singing of songs to the Lord that glorify Him, as well as prayerful words of praise and thanksgiving.)

   _____

   _____

   _____

   _____

   _____

   _____

   _____

   _____

3. Read and study the Bible, the Holy Word of God.

QUESTION: How much time am I willing to spend growing closer in heart knowledge as well as head knowledge to the one who gave His life for me? When and where can I do this daily? (This can include reading the Bible, studying the Bible utilizing respected commentaries for better understanding of scripture, and attending Bible studies and Christian conferences, which are all great ways to learn more of God's word.)

_____

_____

_____

_____

_____

_____

_____

_____

There are also things we can do on a weekly basis to combat battle fatigue and increase our spiritual strength. This includes church services, Bible studies, fellowship, and sharing/seeking counsel with Spirit filled believers.

QUESTION: Have I been faithful and consistent with the above daily and weekly activities? With which ones have I been faithful and consistent? With which ones do I need to become faithful and consistent?

Like the church at Smyrna, Jesus did not bring any accusations against the church of Philadelphia. He commends them for their endurance in the face of much persecution. He encourages them that if they hold on just a little bit longer, they will not have to suffer the hour of trial that will fall upon the earth. What an amazing blessing and promise for them, especially compared to other churches who were specifically told that they were about to suffer!

For us today, we can be thankful that although all of us – believers and unbelievers – will suffer tribulation in this lifetime in this world before Jesus returns, we as believers are not subject to the wrath of God. This will occur after the seventh seal is broken, at the sound of the last trumpet in the Book of Revelation, before God's wrath is poured out upon the world. The Word of God in His Holy Bible assures us of this!

Jesus says that those who overcome will be like columns or pillars in God's temple. In a city prone to earthquakes with the resultant collapse of buildings, overcomers would be the opposite – strong, sturdy, steadfast, never to collapse. Jesus, then, goes on to say that overcomers will live with Him forever in eternity in His permanent city of New Jerusalem! What a wonderful world that will be!!

MORE REFLECTIONS ON CHAPTER SIX

CHAPTER SEVEN
The Church at Laodicea

Revelation 3:14-22 - 14 And unto the angel of the church of the Laodiceans write; These things saith the Amen, the faithful and true witness, the beginning of the creation of God; 15 I know thy works, that thou art neither cold nor hot: I would thou wert cold or hot. 16 So then because thou art lukewarm, and neither cold nor hot, I will spue thee out of my mouth. 17 Because thou sayest, I am rich, and increased with goods, and have need of nothing; and knowest not that thou art wretched, and miserable, and poor, and blind, and naked: 18 I counsel thee to buy of me gold tried in the fire, that thou mayest be rich; and white raiment, that thou mayest be clothed, and [that] the shame of thy nakedness do not appear; and anoint thine eyes with eyesalve, that thou mayest see. 19 As many as I love, I rebuke and chasten: be zealous therefore, and repent. 20 Behold, I stand at the door, and knock: if any man hear my voice, and open the door, I will come in to him, and will sup with him, and he with me. 21 To him that overcometh will I grant to sit with me in my throne, even as I also overcame, and am set down with my Father in his throne. 22 He that hath an ear, let him hear what the Spirit saith unto the churches.

Laodicea was located on a busy trade route forty miles southeast of Philadelphia. Antiochus II named this city after his wife, Laodice. It was a very wealthy city filled with bankers and merchants. Laodicea was a very independent city and was in need of nothing in the natural. After a devastating earthquake in 17 A.D., Laodicea as a whole was so arrogant that they refused financial aid from Rome to assist in its rebuilding because they felt they were above requiring assistance from anyone other than themselves.

Jesus identifies Himself to the believers at Laodicea as the "Amen," which indicates that He is a faithful and true witness, meaning that He never swerves from the truth. He also states that He was with God in the beginning during creation. John 1:3 states that "All things were made through Him [Jesus], and without Him [Jesus] was not anything made that was made." Certainly, the church of Laodicea had no question in their minds from whom this letter came!

Jesus starts His message to them by rebuking the Laodicean church for being lukewarm. As we will see, being lukewarm has dire consequences particularly when it comes to where we will spend our eternity. Sadly, the church of Laodicea received no praise from the Lord, only rebukes and corrections. But Jesus also makes sure that they know that even His rebukes are evidence of His love for them so that they can repent and receive their ultimate salvation.

In that time in history and in that location with its climate, lukewarm or room temperature water was considered dangerous to consume. Cold water suggested fresh water from a spring, while hot water suggested the water had been heated and cleansed. Only hot or cold water was considered safe to consume. As such, telling the believers at Laodicea that they were lukewarm was not a compliment. The truth of the matter was that the church of Laodicea was satisfied with the status quo. Everything was just fine in their eyes and in their own opinion, and they also believed that they were just fine in the eyes of the Lord.

This reminded me of my days before I truly gave my heart and life to the Lord. I was a lifelong practicing catholic. It was not until my early forties when my marriage unexpectedly collapsed that I began to question my faith. I realized that my church participation was little more than a mindless chant and a series of repetitive, predictable movements. I stood, sat, and knelt when everyone else did, and I mindlessly chanted the prayers with the congregation while I was thinking about what I was going to have for lunch when the service was over. But when my life fell apart, all of a sudden it occurred to me that there HAS to be more to God than this! This revelation is what began my journey, and what ultimately resulted in me having a personal relationship with the living God!

These thoughts led me to wonder if, perhaps, the church at Laodicea was in a similar state where their church gatherings had become a series of repetitive activities. Perhaps, in time, there was no longer any thought or heart effort put into any aspect of their activities for the Lord. Certainly, this scenario would be considered lukewarm at best. Enough love of the Lord to go through the motions combined with enough love of the world to not fully commit to the Lord.

> **QUESTION**: Where is my mind and heart, not only when I am at a church service, but throughout my day? When I pray, am I really thinking about what I am saying to the Lord? Am I willing and able to just sit with my mind quiet and respectfully wait for a word from Him at times?

_____

_____

_____

Now that I am following the Lord with all my heart and am hot as a fire for Him, all I want to do is talk about Him and the issues related to Him. I am happiest when I know I am directly serving Him in some manner. I am no longer ashamed or uncomfortable to give thanks to the Lord before I eat a meal with unbelievers, raise my hands in worship, drop to my knees to pray before people, and even pray out loud before others. Since I tend to be more introverted, it took me a while to break free of the shackles of caring what other people thought about me. My born-again friends and family are right with me in all of this, while my non-believing friends and family think I am a "Jesus freak" – which I now see as a great compliment!

The primary focus of my mind and heart shifted from myself to Jesus over this period of time. I would have to say that this was one of the biggest changes in my life. Because my focus changed, so did my heart, attitudes and behaviors. All of this resulted in a whole new and beautiful life.

> **QUESTION**: When I pray, Do I primarily ask God to meet MY needs and desires, even if those desires are fleshly and carnal? Am I only inclined to thank the Lord when He has given me what I wanted?

QUESTION: When I pray, are most of my prayers focused on the salvation and betterment of others? Do I thank the Lord consistently for all that He is and all He has done for me on the cross? Can I still thank Him during those challenging seasons of life?

Your honest answers to these questions will tell you where your heart really is concerning the Lord. This self-reflection is NOT for self-condemnation. This is your opportunity to repent of what needs repenting, and to establish or deepen your personal relationship with the Lord. Your eternity is at stake here! Please take it seriously!

When one thinks of a young couple who are to be married, one thinks of two people who are crazy, madly in love with each other. That is exactly how the bride of Christ is to be: crazy, madly in love with the Lord! Jesus, who was sinless, proved his deep love for us in that He died a horrific death to pay the debt for our sins in order to reconcile us back to Him. I would think it would be quite repugnant for any Bridegroom to watch his bride-to-be walk down the aisle only to have her walk slowly, chat on her phone, and put a hand up to tell him to just wait a minute until she is finished and ready to join Him! That behavior would be lukewarm and downright rude, at best.

An example of lukewarm behavior in a believer's life would be when they remain distracted by their cell phone and other matters of life when their entire focus should be on the Lord for prayer, praise, worship, and learning. It is no wonder the Lord will spue the lukewarm Christians out of His mouth! Our Lord and Savior deserves nothing less than our entire heart and our very best!

This leads me to want to address public praise and worship of our Lord and Savior. There are so many beautiful songs that we sing in church services to give glory to the Lord. To assess which songs truly give God glory, I would say that if we can substitute our spouse's name in the song for the name of the Lord and the song still makes sense, then that song is not worthy to be considered a worship song for the Lord. It might be a pretty love song, but such a song is in no way to be considered worthy to give glory to the Lamb of God who took away the sins of the world! The point here is that our public praise and worship can also be or become lukewarm if we are not careful.

QUESTION: What are my expectations for praise and worship particularly during a church service? Do I wait to be entertained by what appears to be a concert at church, substituting fleshly hype for a true encounter with the Holy Spirit?

___

___

___

___

___

___

___

___

___

Hype can be viewed as a "really good show" with lots of bling and energy. Some churches have choreographed dance-like movements, mist machines, and excessively loud volume to almost mimic a secular rock concert, in order to attract parishioners or fans, as the case may be. The focus is on the performance, not the Lord, thus making the worship lukewarm even though it might appear energetic superficially.

In Holy Spirit filled worship, one might see the worship team break the flow of the music to either change the song to accommodate the leading of the Holy Spirit or to interject scripture and/or prayer as they are led. When the Holy Spirit is leading and our hearts are in tune to Him, many worshippers feel the unction to raise their hands in praise, drop to their knees, shed tears, or trail off into personal prayer. This is what true, on-fire worship to the Lord looks like! Truly the level of energy of the music played, whether a fast beat song of praise versus a beautiful slow hymn, would elicit the same response from those worshipping. Regardless of song style, our hearts are deeply touched and our love for the Lord just bubbles over when the worship is Spirit filled and focused on the Lord!

> **QUESTION**: Am I truly engaging my heart in worship or am I just singing a song?

_____
_____
_____
_____
_____
_____
_____

> **QUESTION**: Do I ever feel compelled to raise my hands in worship, trail off into fervent prayer, fall to my knees, or even shed tears during worship? Do I willingly follow these promptings of the Holy Spirit, or do I quench the Holy Spirit in fear of what the people nearby might think of me?

_____
_____
_____
_____

Scripture warns us that we cannot serve two masters. In other words, we are either people pleasers or we are God pleasers. We cannot do both, and that is a choice each one of us must make individually.

People who are lukewarm Christians typically have enough head knowledge about God and the Christian faith to understand and talk about Jesus Christ, and they may even believe in Him. But they lack deep faith in their heart to be fully engaged with the Lord and saved. But scripture warns us that the devil and his demons also believe in Jesus, yet their eternity in the lake of fire is already sealed! (See James 2:19; Revelation 20:10.)

> **QUESTION**: Am I hot, cold, or lukewarm for Christ? Why do I believe this is my current status before the Lord? Does my behavior and manner of speech indicate that I may be in error about my initial conclusion? Would those around me say that I am hot, cold, or lukewarm for Christ?

Some might think that this "all or nothing" proposal is a bit extreme. Let's look at it from a natural perspective. Let's say you are very much in love and soon to be married. You are at the alter and just finished saying your vows to your soon to be spouse. Your spouse now speaks their vows to you, vowing to be 100% faithful to you for only 364 days of each year you are together. How would that make you feel? Would you go through with the wedding? Why would our Lord and Savior expect any less than 100% faithfulness from us?

Getting back to the original scripture regarding Laodicea, Jesus states He will spue the lukewarm Christians out of His mouth. What does this mean? In the Greek, it actually means to "forcefully vomit" out of one's mouth. In other words, Jesus finds the lukewarm Christian to be quite vile and distasteful, and He will forcefully remove them from His presence. That's intense!

Moreover, Jesus points out that His opinion of the believers in Laodicea is vastly different than their view of themselves. They see themselves as rich, prosperous, awesome, and self-sufficient. But the Lord sees them as poor and pitiful! Rabbis often used the term "rich" to denote righteousness and "poor" to denote wickedness. The Lord was not referring to their condition in the natural, but to their spiritual condition. The Lord found them to be spiritually lacking, and He points out that the Laodiceans were incredibly self-deceived in their assessment of themselves.

In Matthew 15:7-8 Jesus states, "Ye hypocrites, well did Esaias prophesy of you, saying, this people draweth nigh unto me with their lips; but their heart is far from me." James 1:22 also states, "But be ye doers of the word, and not hearers only, deceiving your own selves."

These two scriptures point out that the Lord is primarily concerned with our heart attitudes. If our hearts are fully focused upon the Lord, our behaviors will change accordingly out of love for Him. Our works of love and obedience to the Lord will ultimately change the optics of our lives to others, and they will notice that change.

In James chapter 2, he mentions that faith without works is dead. Although our works do not save us, because we are only saved by grace through faith in Christ, it is through our works born out of love for Christ that others will know us by our "fruits" or changed behaviors. Perhaps, the Laodiceans went through all the religious motions expected of them so that they appeared godly on the outside, but the inside of their heart and their motivations were very far from the Lord, and they could not tell the difference.

> **QUESTION**: Where is my heart concerning the Lord? Am I motivated to do good works for the Lord out of my love for Him or, perhaps, could it be out of my love of the praise of man? This could be the most important question here: what motivates me to do these good works?

_____

_____

_____

_____

_____

_____

_____

_____

_____

_____

Please, don't pass on answering this question! Read it again and ask the Lord to show you how He sees you! It is truly His desire that NONE be lost to Him and that ALL would receive salvation! That means you, too. In His immense mercy and patience, He provides ample time for us to repent and turn away from sin (including our lukewarmness) in order to be reconciled back to Him.

But the repenting is our own choice! The Lord never takes away our free will. This said, our choices here on earth are what determine our eternal destination: eternity in heaven with the Lord or separated from Him in hell forever.

We all have a choice to make, and making no choice is actually a choice in the eyes of the Lord. The Lord created man with the ability to choose to fully follow and love Him, or not. Love has so much more meaning when someone chooses to willingly love and serve you versus being forced to love and serve you.

The ONLY way to be saved is to be filled with the Holy Spirit of the living God. We must invite the Holy Spirit into our heart and ask Him to be the Lord (Master) of our lives. When the Holy Spirit resides in us, the Lord sees His reflection in us when He gazes upon us, indicating that we truly belong to Him.

In John 14:16-17, Jesus adds, "I will ask my Father. He will give you another one to help you and be with you always. He will send you the Spirit of truth. The world cannot receive the true Spirit because it does not see or know Him. You know Him because He is with you and will be in you." This speaks of the wonderful close relationship we have with the living God once His Spirit lives inside us, and we are saved and truly His. Once the Holy Spirit dwells within us, we must willingly submit to His promptings out of our love for Him.

God's Word says in John 15:15, "If you love me, you will obey Me." The Holy Spirit working in conjunction with our desire to be fully obedient to the Lord gives us the power to overcome sin. It is through this close relationship that our hearts are changed, which results in our behaviors and our lives being changed. Sure, we may still have the fleshly desire to want to sin, but our love for the Lord should far surpass that fleshly desire.

> *Matthew 16:24-26 [Jesus speaking] 'If any man will come after Me, let him deny himself, and take up his cross, and follow Me. For whosoever will save his [earthly] life shall lose it [eternal life]: and whosoever will lose his [earthly] life for My sake shall find it [eternal life]. For what is a man profited, if he shall gain the whole world, and lose his own soul? Or what shall a man give in exchange for his soul?*

I would say that Matthew 16:24-26 states the Lord's expectations of those who follow Him very clearly. We are to live obedient and sacrificial lives unto the Lord with the help of His Holy Spirit in order to obtain the reward of eternal life with Him in heaven. It truly is just that plain and simple!

> **QUESTION**: Have I fully submitted myself to the Lord, or do I only submit to the commandments I agree with and/or those directives that don't really cost me anything here on earth? Is there something (an object, a behavior, a relationship, an activity, etc.) that I am still holding onto which the Lord desires that I let go of or stop?

Please take your time and prayerfully consider what the Lord may be trying to show you now.

In the next portion of Jesus' letter to Laodicea, He makes a reference to the main exports of that city which were gold, garments, and eye salve. Jesus advises them to buy gold from Him. In 1 Peter 1:7, Peter describes faith which has been proven genuine through the tests of fire (adversities of life) as being far more valuable than gold. In other words, this church needed to place their faith in Jesus with its eternal rewards instead of placing their faith in their earthly riches with its temporary rewards.

Jesus describes the Laodicean church as being, "naked" spiritually, meaning they were clothed in unrighteousness instead of righteousness. Jesus offered them garments of white to cover their spiritual nakedness. In other words, Jesus was offering them the opportunity to become righteous before Him and have eternal life through His grace by their faith in Him.

Jesus also described the Laodicean church as being spiritually "blind," indicating that they were unable to see their darkened, unrighteous spiritual state. Jesus offered them eye salve that could cure their spiritual "blindness" so they could see their true spiritual state before Him. If the Laodicean church accepted what Jesus was offering them symbolically, they would be able to see their lukewarm condition, repent, and be reconciled to Him.

Jesus then adds that those whom He loves, He reproves and disciplines. When the Lord corrects us, we feel convicted. We may feel saddened that we displeased the Lord in some manner but our love for Him motivates us to repent and change as needed. But just like any good parent, the Lord's correction is provided out of love for us, so that we can repent and change our behavior for our ultimate good. Truly, if a parent did not love their child, correction would never be provided because the parent really does not care about their child's well-being.

Therefore, we can take heart when the Lord corrects us, as it is one of the many ways that He continues to show His love for us! On the other hand, condemnation is when we feel very bad about ourselves regardless of whether or not we have remorse for our actions. Condemnation and even self-accusing thoughts come from the enemy. The evil one's purpose is always to weaken our walk with the Lord. Believers beware!

In all of this, including His correction, the Lord is always a perfect gentleman. He will never force Himself upon anyone. He always allows us to exercise our free will. This said, the Lord went to the cross for everyone on the earth to believe and be saved. It is totally up to each individual person to choose to fully accept or reject the Lord and what He has done for us. There is no middle ground. His Holy Spirit will only enter an individual when a person truly believes that Jesus is Lord and that God raised Him from the dead.

Every person has equal opportunity for salvation and eternal life in Christ Jesus. The ball is in our court! Jesus is patiently waiting for you to invite Him to be your Lord and Savior. However, there will come a time either at our physical death or at the end of this age when the window of opportunity will close. Just like the door to Noah's Ark was shut and sealed before the judgment of the flood poured out on the earth, the open door of salvation through faith in Jesus will be closed before the wrath of God is poured out in the final day of judgment. Then, it will be too late. Your choice will have been made and your eternal fate sealed.

Jesus concludes His letter to Laodicea by telling them that He is patiently and gently seeking each and every one of them (us) to offer them (us) the gift of eternal salvation. He states that He stands and knocks at the door indicating that He patiently waits for our response to His callings. Jesus promises that if any man hears, i.e. considers, his unrighteous state and opens the door, i.e. calls on the name of Jesus, Jesus will answer! Jesus answers by sending His Holy Spirit to pardon our sins and love us freely.

But this is just the beginning of a wonderful and new life in Christ! The Holy Spirit then works in conjunction with our voluntary desire to submit unto the Lord in order to fashion each and every one of us into a new creature in Christ. Our heart's desires, the motivations of our heart, our behaviors, and ultimately our lives will be changed on this earth to more and more reflect Jesus!

But that is not all! The ultimate reward for those of us who choose to love, follow, and obey Jesus is eternal life spent with Him in paradise! Amen!

More Reflections on Chapter Seven

FINAL REFLECTIONS

I am not going to end this book with what is commonly referred to as "the sinner's prayer." Why? Because if you are reading this, you are most likely already a believer. The letters of Revelation were written to believers in the churches, just like this book has been. Moreover, that "sinner's prayer" has been said by countless people throughout the years as some sort of magic word combination that automatically will turn you into a saved, born again Christian. It does not work that way!

Jesus does not want mere lip service and fixed, mechanical prayers. He wants your full heart! He must be first in your heart and your life. If you really mean it in your heart, you will tolerate no other gods or idols in your life. He deserves nothing less! Jesus Christ gave His all for each and every one of us on that cross. The least we can do is give our all to Him!

Rather than cite a scripted prayer, I would prefer that you ponder all that the Lord has done for you and formulate your own, individual, heart-felt prayer to the Lord.

First of all, please know that the Lord intentionally created and desired you – YOU! He intentionally loved you so much that He chose to give you free will to either choose Him and His gift of eternal life or reject Him. Close your eyes and contemplate the love the Lord has for you. He made you uniquely different from every other human being throughout history for His good pleasure. He knows your strengths and weaknesses, and all you have ever or will ever say, think, and do. And He still chose you! He loves YOU!

Now, contemplate what Jesus as the Lamb of God did on that

cross so that your sins could be forgiven. Old Testament Law, set forth by God, dictated that there must be a blood sacrifice to atone for the sins of man. At that time, traditional animal sacrifice needed to be done over and over as the shedding of animal blood could only temporarily provide forgiveness for the sins of man.

Since Jesus is God enrobed in flesh, ONLY He could be the perfect and final blood sacrifice for the ultimate forgiveness of the sins of man. I want you to know that Jesus was beaten and whipped so badly that not only was He unrecognizable as Jesus of Nazareth on that cross, but He was unrecognizable as a human being! Think about that!! And if you were the only person ever created upon this earth, Jesus would have gone to the cross for just you alone! Close your eyes and contemplate all of this.

Jesus gave absolutely everything on that cross to reconcile His creation back unto Himself. He had to eradicate the sin of His beloved creation because it was our sin that kept us separated from Him. God cannot be in the presence of sin. God did what He had to do to give each of us the opportunity to be reconciled back to Him and spend all eternity with Him as He always intended. That choice is ours to make.

The purpose of this devotional has been to provide each of you the opportunity to pray and look into your hearts to make sure you are righteous before our Lord and Savior. The goal was to provide an understandable and practical manner in which to do so.

We have an opportunity to self-reflect, pray, repent of what needs repenting, and enhance that which is pleasing to our Lord. The Lord would have it that none be lost! For God so loved the world...

My final prayer is that I get to meet all of you one day in Heaven where we can raise our voices all together and give glory to our wonderful Lord and Savior, Jesus! Amen.

A CALL TO THE ROMANS ROAD

ROMANS 3:10
"As it is written: 'There is no one righteous, not even one.'"

ROMANS 3:23
"For all have sinned and fall short of the glory of God."

ROMANS 6:23
"For the wages of sin is death but the gift of God is eternal life in Christ Jesus our Lord."

ROMANS 5:8
"But God demonstrates His own love for us in this: While we were still sinners, Christ died for us."

ROMANS 10:9-10, 13
"If you declare with your mouth 'Jesus is Lord,' and believe in your heart that God raised Him from the dead, you will be saved. For it is with your heart that you believe and are justified, and it is with your mouth that you profess your faith and are saved."

ROMANS 5:1-2
"Therefore, since we have been justified through faith, we have peace with God through our Lord Jesus Christ, through whom we have gained access by faith into His grace in which we now stand."

ROMANS 8:1
"Therefore, there is now no condemnation for those who are in Christ Jesus."

ABOUT THE AUTHOR

For as long as she can remember, Catherine Vitetta always loved her Lord and Savior, Jesus. Catherine and her husband, George, had a home church with multiple small community outreaches until George went to be with the Lord in 2022. Now, she is going even deeper in her relationship with the Lord by serving Him in new and unexpected ways, including writing this book! It is Catherine's desire that this book will draw each reader into a more intimate relationship with Jesus so that they too can experience the love, peace, and joy that she has found in Him.

ABOUT MANIFEST PUBLICATIONS

Manifest Publications is the publishing division of Manifest International, LLC. Our objective is to help like-minded ministries and writers produce and distribute materials which proclaim Jesus Christ to all the world and equip the global Church for unity and maturity.

www.manifestinternational.com